Dead Dreams
Can Live!

Other books by David Matthew:

Christian Manhood
(School of the Word/Harvestime)

Church Adrift
(Marshall Pickering)

Dead Dreams Can Live!

Your hopes fulfilled

David Matthew

Harvestime

Scripture quotations are generally taken from the New International Version. Copyright © 1978 by the New York International Bible Society and published by Hodder & Stoughton. Used by permission.

ISBN 0 947714 19 7

Typeset in the United Kingdom by: Harvestime Services Ltd, 136 Hall Lane, Bradford West Yorkshire BD4 7DG
Printed by: The Bath Press, Lower Bristol Road, Bath BA2 3BL

Contents

To Jonathan

who cherishes his dream of tomorrow
yet lives as a man of God today

Introduction

It's no insult to be called a dreamer. Jesus was one. It was 'for the joy set before him' that he 'endured the cross, scorning its shame'.

The heroes of faith catalogued in Hebrews 11 were dreamers, too. Forever hankering after the ideals rough-sketched in the promises of God, they 'saw them and welcomed them from a distance'.

Dreams are like grappling irons. We throw them up ahead to where we want to be, then heave on the rope to get there.

Let's be clear, though, that by 'dream' I don't mean any old mental fantasy. I mean the dream implanted by God in the heart of every Christian, the dream of being used by him in the outworking of his eternal purpose.

In practice that spells something different for each of us. To one it may be raising a family for God. To another, breaking open new ground with the gospel in some far-flung corner of the earth. To another, publishing Christian books, or making money for the kingdom, or shepherding God's flock, or becoming a prayer-warrior, or composing songs of praise and worship. The variations are endless.

All our dreams, however, have the habit of burning bright for a while, only to die down rapidly to a faint ember. Things don't work out the way we anticipated. Doubts set in, and the dream is written off as a flash of fantasy and then forgotten.

I have written this book to encourage you to hold on to the dream God gave you. It comes partly out of personal experience and partly from the ups and downs of that classic dreamer and my favourite Bible character: Joseph.

'Hold on to the dream God gave you' is my message. But you will also find me urging you to let it die – so that it can realise maximum potential by resurrection. An intriguing paradox, you think? Read on, and all will become clear!

You will find what follows especially relevant if your dream concerns some form of full-time Christian ministry. But the life-principles outlined remain of value and relevance to every child of God – including you – and to every God-given dream.

May your life be touched as you read.

David Matthew

September 1986

I dream all the time and suddenly it's true.

Joe Johnson,
new World Snooker Champion, 1986

Joseph . . . was sold for a servant. His feet they hurt with fetters, he was laid in chains of iron . . . . Until his word [to his cruel brothers] came true, the word of the Lord tried and tested him.

Psalm 105:17-19
(Amplified Bible)

CHAPTER 1

Checking out your dream

We all have dreams. They may be the result of eating a cheese sandwich for supper, or they may be straight from heaven.

Even animals have dreams, it appears. I have often watched our family dog, fast asleep in front of the fire, begin twitching and squeaking, apparently chasing a cat down the streets of his doggy dreamworld!

Dreams of this kind are usually a jumbled-up replay of bits and pieces of mental film. It's like a sleeping computer having a hiccup and churning out a hotchpotch of unrelated data on to its screen.

Not that we should regard all our dreams as nonsense. Psychologists have delved deep into the subject, assuring us that many dreams reflect our subconscious hopes, fears, aspirations and insecurities, all wrapped up in the picture language of everyday experience.

Not surprisingly, followers of the occult have been quick to exploit this aspect of life. To browse along the shelves of any 'alternative' bookshop is to find a whole range of writings on the interpretation of dreams, with suggested links into the realm of the occult and the alleged influence of the stars.

Something to Live For

What we are chiefly concerned with in this book, however, is dreams in the wider sense. When Martin Luther King proclaimed, 'I have a dream', he wasn't referring to the pictures in his mind while asleep. He was using the term more in the sense of 'vision'. He had a consuming desire to see the black people of the USA fully integrated into society, with equal rights and standing alongside white people. That was his dream, his burning ambition.

For some people, of course, a similar vision or ambition does grow out of a literal dream. Joseph's belief that he was destined for power and leadership came that way (Genesis 37:5-10). And since then, many Christians have embarked upon a life's work for God as the result of a vivid dream (while sleeping) or an equally vivid vision (a waking 'dream').

But for most of us, dreams in the wider sense of the term form more gradually. We find a growing conviction in our hearts regarding our future role in the purpose of God.

Like faith, such a conviction usually just 'comes' (Romans 10:17). We gradually become aware of its presence in our heart and then turn to examine it more closely. It's not a matter of, 'Today I think I'll cook up some dreams and settle upon a goal for my life.' No, we focus more sharply on what is already there.

Andy, a friend of mine, is a typical case. For years he worked very successfully in insurance. During that time his dream of full-time involvement in pastoral ministry became more and more clear until eventually, in his late thirties, he reached full conviction about it. He resigned from his job (with a very warm and appreciative send-off by his colleagues) and enrolled in Bible college with the blessing of his local church elders.

Dreams: A Necessity

Andy's dream took a long time to crystallise. Yours may come faster, maybe overnight. But one thing is true of us all: *without dreams we cannot live.* 'Where there is no vision, the people perish' (Proverbs 29:18 KJV).

Dreams give purpose to life, lifting our sights above the ordinariness of everyday affairs and giving us direction, like the sailor who looks up from the heaving deck of his ship to set his course by the stars.

Without dreams, the humdrum of life, routine, harsh circumstances and annoying people become unbearable. Men without dreams are prone to nervous breakdown, bodily sickness and dullness of mind. They have no sense of adventure, no purposeful glint in the eye, no drive.

Tell me, what is *your* dream? What is it that first captured your heart, perhaps years ago, and inspired you to action in order to see it fulfilled?

And what has happened to that dream since then? Has its ability to inspire you remained or faded? Have you become a little cynical with the passage of time and the pressure of hard circumstances? Have you, perhaps, even written off your dream as wishful thinking or crazy youthful idealism and dug in for a long, hard slog of routine for the rest of your life?

In a word, has the dream *died?*

Is it from God?

Now is a good time to return to the dream and check it out. Start with this basic question: 'Is my dream from God or not?'

If you can just get the answer to that one, everything else will become clear. Because if your dream *is* from God, there's only one thing you can do: hold on to it! But if it's no more than fantasising or wishful thinking, you can drop it at once and ask the Lord to implant *his* dream in your heart in its place.

One thing you can be sure of: *God does have a dream for you.* It was he, after all, who made you, and he knows that, for humankind, to have no dream is to stagnate.

Open your spiritual ears, then, to hear from the Lord. If the dream you once had is now fulfilled, ask him for a new one. You may have dreamed of being married and now your dream is a reality. Say, 'Lord, where do you want me to go from here?

What's the next goal for me?'

You may be facing the particular difficulties labelled by psychologists 'the mid-life crisis'. Somewhere between the ages of 40 and 55 many people, Christians included, go through such a crisis.

'Have I missed my way?' they ask themselves. 'Am I over the hill and redundant to God?' Or, if they came to Christ late in life: 'If only I'd been saved earlier, I could have devoted my life to serving the Lord. But now it's too late; my best years are gone for ever, all wasted on selfish, godless activity.'

With God it's *never* too late! You will never be over the hill as far as he is concerned, and certainly you will never be redundant to him – unless, of course, you *believe* you will, in which case it might as well be true, because the results in terms of despair will be the same.

I don't care if you are 99, if you have just come to Christ or if you have frittered away your Christian life right up to today. God still wants to implant a dream in your heart!

Open up to him right now. Ask him to take care of the past, then turn your eyes towards the future and pray, 'Lord, please show me the way forward, give me a sense of direction, implant your dream.'

If that's what you need to do, put this book aside without delay and do it now!

For many of us this won't be necessary because we already have our dream. Our need is to discover whether or not it is from God. How, then, do you check out your dream?

Giving God Credit

For a start, since you are (I hope) a Spirit-filled Christian, submitted to the Lord in body, mind and spirit, why not begin by *assuming that the dream comes from him?* It seems reasonable, after all, to give more credit to God than to your own wishful thinking or to the confusing tactics of the devil.

So tell him, 'Lord, I'm assuming that this dream of mine, this conviction about my future, is from you. If it's not, Lord, please cause it to fade rapidly, but if it *is* from you, please strengthen it and confirm it within me, so that I'm left in no doubt.'

The Lord will soon make things clear. He can't resist the prayer of the man or woman intent on knowing and doing his will.

Something Desirable

Another pointer is this: the dream will be something you *want.* Though at present it may seem way beyond your reach, you will nevertheless desire it strongly and be unable to shake the desire off.

Again, assume that God is in it. Don't be like the young man who once talked to me about promotion in his job. 'I know it can't be God's will,' he remarked sadly, 'because it's something I want.'

What a strange concept of our heavenly Father! Why should our desire and his will be thought incompatible? It's like the old idea that if a cough medicine tastes nice it can't be much good, or that school-children will never really learn anything if the lessons are enjoyable. How ridiculous!

'Delight yourself in the Lord,' advised King David, 'and he will give you the *desires* of your heart' (Psalm 37:4).

To delight yourself in the Lord is to enjoy his company, to take pleasure in your walk with him. It is to 'seek first his kingdom and his righteousness' (Matthew 6:33). It is to be first and foremost a Christian, with your sights set on pleasing the Lord.

The fact that you may not have been a Christian very long is irrelevant. If God is Number One in your life, that's all that matters. It's not a question of how far you have travelled along the road to Christian maturity but of whether you are moving in the right direction. If you are, then you can be said to be delighting yourself in the Lord and you qualify for the promise!

Do you realise that, no matter how long you have been a believer, you 'participate in the divine nature' anyway (2 Peter 1:4)? Your basic tendency now is to be Godlike, for the 'divine sperm' is in you (1 John 3:9 literally). God's very own life – his genes, we might say – are at work in you, causing you to grow more and more like your Father!

With this divinely-given head start, it's even more certain that as you go on actively to delight yourself in the Lord, your desires will more and more reflect his own desires. What *you* want will increasingly reflect what *he* wants.

Look at your dream that way. Whatever it is, could it be that you want it because he himself wants it and has placed it in your heart? Assume the answer to be yes.

Obstacles are Normal!

One line of reasoning you should *not* follow is this: 'I really thought my dream was from God, but even though I pressed hard for its fulfilment it didn't work out. So clearly I was mistaken.'

No! It doesn't follow that if a dream 'dies' it was never from God. In fact I would say the very opposite: in the light of both Scripture and experience, a God-given dream usually *has* to die before there can be a fulfilment! The grain of wheat must fall into the ground and die before it can bring forth fruit.

We sometimes have a simplistic idea that if God is in a scheme it will all click miraculously into place as a token of his approval, but that if problems arise it's a sure sign we have got our guidance wrong.

Nothing could be further from the truth. Sure, God can, and sometimes does, cause everything to fall conveniently into place for us, but, as we shall see, he more often permits difficulties to cross our path.

So if you have dropped your dream just because it didn't work out the way you expected, pick it up again and hold on to it while we consider God's ways more closely. There's hope for you yet!

Now let's summarise. God has a dream for you. He is anxious to make it known. It will be something you desire. And the chances are that obstacles will stand in the way of its fulfilment.

Does that make sense to you? Does it match up to your own experience? It does? Then together let's pursue the matter further.

CHAPTER 2

The things
that go wrong

My own dream began to form when I was
about 13, not long after I was saved. It became much clearer when, at the age of 17, I
was gloriously filled with the Holy Spirit. I
just knew somehow that I was going to be a
full-time servant of the Lord. It was my des-
tiny, I believed, to bless many thousands of
people in a ministry that would cross international boundaries.

Maybe it sounds a bit ambitious, but that's
simply what the dream was, and there's no
doubt about it – it was from God. God im-
plants many dreams in the time of youth, so
that the seeds can take hold in the fertile soil
of youthful zeal. That way, the weeds of
cynicism and sophistication, which grow

with age, are prevented from smothering the tender plant.

Don't write off your youthful vision. It was at the age of 17 that Joseph heard from God. He correctly deduced from the dreams of sheaves of corn and of sun, moon and stars bowing down to him that he was destined to play a prominent leadership role in his family.*

No Trumpeting!

Joseph wasn't very wise, however, in the way he handled his dreams. He talked about them cockily to his older brothers and strutted around in the richly ornamented robe his father had given him, which was a sign of special approval and was seen by Joseph as a token that he was already on his way towards leadership in the family. Little wonder his brothers disliked him!

Don't make the same mistake yourself. Be like Mary, the mother of Jesus, who, when given the most tremendous promise by an

---

* You can read the story of Joseph in Genesis 37 to 50. As he will be referred to often in this book, you would benefit from being familiar with the outline of his life.

angel of the Lord, wisely shared it only with a trusted friend and relative. Even when it all began to happen, she 'treasured up all these things and pondered them in her heart' (Luke 2:19).

Hold *your* dream in your heart, sharing it wisely and humbly only with those who you know will pray, understand and encourage you rather than be threatened by it or trumpet it all around.

When Things Go Wrong

Now let's look at the way dreams tend to die. We will leave until a later stage the important question of *why* things go wrong and first focus our attention on *what* goes wrong.

The main culprit here seems to be *circumstances.* Agreed?

Having a firm grasp of the vision God has given, we imagine that events will slip into place so that it can be fulfilled smoothly and quickly. But we're invariably disappointed.

It wouldn't be so bad if circumstances remained neutral, neither favouring nor hindering the dream's fulfilment. At least then we'd be able to push through. But it rarely seems to work out that way. Instead, the circumstances somehow seem to militate *against* the dream's outworking!

'I've already noticed that!' you remark.

So have I. Infuriating, isn't it?

This was certainly my own experience. During my student years, some time after the formation of my dream, I came to believe that God was calling me to missionary work in Peru. So, happily married and with my course completed, I fully expected the doors to open to South America.

My wife and I approached missionary organisations. We wrote to people in Peru. We visited Peruvian missionaries on furlough. In fact we pushed every Peruvian door we could find, but all our efforts proved in vain.

Then, to cap it all, family circumstances changed. My wife had been brought up by her grandparents, and all along we had felt a special responsibility to repay them for their kindness, especially in their old age. Now they both became quite sick and dependent on us for day-to-day care. How could we possibly leave them stranded?

Who's to Blame?

As you know, there are obstacles and obstacles. Some of them, thrown across our path by the enemy, are to be overcome by faith and holy determination. Others are *God's* obstacles, thrust before us by a higher wisdom for our ultimate good, and we attack such obstacles at our peril.

Somehow, my wife and I just knew that our obstacles were from God. He was the one engineering circumstances to block our headlong rush to the rescue of the Peruvian Indians.

How strange! And how impossible to understand! Why should the Lord inspire us with a dream only to block the path to its fulfilment? His love we never doubted, but he seemed to have a peculiar way of showing it!

Perhaps you're feeling like that right now. Take heart – it's normal.

'But some of my circumstances are really awful,' you retort. 'How can you suggest that they come from the hand of a loving God when they bear all the hallmarks of evil?'

Don't forget that Satan is limited. Prowling around looking for someone to devour he may be, but it won't be you – unless you invite him, of course.

The story of Job makes it abundantly clear that the devil can do nothing to you without God's express permission. What's more, the right attitude on your part can actually turn the bad times to your advantage! So even if some of your circumstances have a devilish flavour, it is only because the Lord knows that you can strike a blow at Satan by milking those circumstances of their potential blessing.

God and Satan, remember, are not equals. God is firmly in charge, and he's *for* you, not against you. Take courage!

In Good Company

In fact, your dream-defying problems place you in good biblical company.

Consider Joseph for a moment. Were his dreams of family leadership from God? Most certainly. Then why, just when his course seemed set fair, did things go so drastically wrong?

Recall what happened. His brothers first threw him into an empty water cistern, scaring him half to death as they planned his murder. Then, thinking better of it, they sold him to some passing traders who carried him far away from the family he was destined to lead, right down to Egypt, where he was sold as a slave!

The dream promised *leadership;* the circumstances provided *slavery.* The two are complete opposites!

It was the same with Moses. His dream was to deliver his fellow-Israelites from bondage in Egypt – and the dream was from God. But as soon as Moses began to act on the dream by taking the part of an Israelite in dispute with an Egyptian, things went radically wrong. He ended up fleeing the country as a fugitive and taking up sheep-farming in Midian, miles away from the very people the dream told him he would rescue. How odd!

Abraham fared little better. It was very nice to be told by God that he would be the father of many nations, but all the circumstances proclaimed otherwise. He and Sarah were childless and, what's more, they were both near-centenarians. Abraham's dream seemed to die circumstantially almost as soon as it was born! Like yours, perhaps?

Still More Setbacks

Then something else tends to happen. As if the initial circumstantial battering isn't enough, the adverse circumstances always seem to be *repeated.* Apparently God isn't content to give the dream a knockout blow; he seems determined to kill it stone dead!

Poor Joseph! Being sold as a slave had been bad enough, but just when things were taking a turn for the better he was struck by a bolt from the blue even more severe: he was thrown into prison!

It wouldn't have been quite so bad if, through some slip-up, he had *deserved* to be jailed. But he wasn't guilty of even the most petty crime. In fact his behaviour had been exemplary: he had firmly yet courteously stuck to his moral principles in the face of re-peated attempts by his master's wife to lure him into her bed.

God must have been very pleased indeed with such a righteous moral stand. If we had been God we would no doubt have re-warded Joseph in some way – fixing a prom-otion or steering some extra cash in his di-rection, perhaps, or bringing the seductive woman to a place of true repentance and faith.

But what actually happened? She turned sour, told lies about Joseph to her husband, and our hero finished up behind bars!

'Where's God in all this?' he might well

have complained. 'What kind of reward is this for my faithfulness and high morality? And as for my dream, how on earth can I ever see it fulfilled under lock and key? What went wrong? Were my dreams just "cheese dreams" after all?'

Understanding God's Ways

Similar questions have probably crossed your own mind, if not your lips. You have done everything right. You have remained faithful to the Lord and to his Word, often under severe pressure. You have done your best to overcome evil with good.

And the result? Major circumstantial difficulties, and any likelihood of your dream's being fulfilled apparently growing more remote by the minute!

Don't despair! It's just that you don't know God and his ways as well as you thought. The renewing of your mind according to his Word (Romans 12:2) isn't as far advanced as you believed. Simply reading this chapter, however, has moved you a little further along the road.

The main thing is that God *was* with

Joseph, even in his hard and puzzling cir-cumstances. He's with you, too, even though it might not seem like it right now.

Joseph believed God and held on to his dream. Be encouraged, and hold on to yours!

CHAPTER 3

People who disappoint

'Teaching would be a marvellous job if only there were no children!' exclaimed one prickly teacher at the end of a bad day.

Your complaint might be similar: 'It would be a lot easier to do the will of God and realise my dreams if only *people* didn't get in the way!' But just as a school is full of children, so the world is full of people, and as often as not they figure prominently in the death of a dream.

People will be a particular problem to you if you are the idealistic type. The great thing about ideals is that they inspire, they uplift, they are gloriously clear and unclouded. But people . . . !

Pricking the Balloon

For a start, people answer back. They pick holes in your noble ideals – that's if they understand them in the first place! People are so earthy, so bound to the material world, whereas your ideals soar like an eagle in the higher, more rarified atmosphere of concepts and ideas.

As it is, God fixed the world so that it's full of people, and for you to try living as if things were otherwise is foolish. Far better to accept the fact and learn to like them. God will use them to keep your feet on the ground, if nothing else!

But even if you're a great lover of people already, you will still find them prominent in the death of your dream. It happens in several ways. From some you will face direct *opposition.* They will appear to take a fiendish delight in putting the squeeze on all your plans and dreams. Like a driving instructor in a dual- control car, whenever you want to put your foot down they'll slam on the brake!

Do you have 'friends' like that? They claim to be 'realists', implying that you yourself are a superspiritual lunatic and your dream a flight of unrestrained fantasy. 'I have the

ministry of counselling caution' is how one
of them described it!

The Power of Jealousy

With such people, jealousy often lurks in the
background. They may be jealous of your
gifts.

This, I feel sure, was the case with Joseph's
brothers. Sensing his leadership ability,
which was beginning to show itself even at
the tender age of 17, they felt threatened,
especially as he was younger than them. So
they conspired to remove this thorn in their
flesh: 'Come now, let's kill him and throw
him into one of these cisterns and say that a
ferocious animal devoured him. Then we'll
see what comes of his dreams.'

Do you have 'brothers' like that?

Or it may be jealousy of your *circumstances* – the favourable circumstances
that seem to equip you for the fulfilment of
your dream.

With Joseph it was the special favour
shown by his father, Jacob. Joseph couldn't
help it, poor fellow. He didn't choose to be
the child of Jacob's old age and the first to be
born to his favourite wife, Rachel. But he no

doubt enjoyed the special attention and he was certainly proud of that richly ornamented robe presented by his father. And why not? Didn't all these circumstances point in the direction of his dream's fulfilment?

The fact that Joseph was responsible for neither his gifts nor his circumstances did nothing to temper the bitterness of his brothers. It hit him with full force: 'When his brothers saw that their father loved him more than any of them, they hated him and could not speak a kind word to him.'

Ashamed of Your Blessings?

This kind of jealous opposition is hard to take – isn't it? I frequently came across supposedly godly people who bitterly opposed me, and I noticed that they were jealous of factors over which I had no control.

I was blessed with fine Christian parents and a stable background. 'Oh yes, it's OK for some,' they implied. 'You may have had a head start on the rest of us, but we'll do our best to see that you don't capitalise on it!'

I also won a scholarship to a good school

and received an excellent academic education. 'You think you're somebody just because you went to that school,' they sneered, 'but we'll bring you down a peg or two and prove that we're just as useful to God as you are!'

I never disputed it for a moment, but their *attitude* hurt.

Before long, such opposition makes you ashamed of your gifts and your circumstances, and you attempt awkwardly to play them down, or even hide them altogether.

What a tragedy! We don't want to swing to the opposite extreme and boast about our gifts and circumstances, but why should we become apologetic either?

Do you have distinct, God-given gifts? Then use them, wisely and sensitively. Never hide them away for fear of jealous criticism. Has God blessed you in your circumstances? Then capitalise on the experience thus placed within your reach, and humbly rejoice in the blessing of God 'who works out everything in conformity with the purpose of his will' (Ephesians 1:11).

Leaders Under Threat

Be particularly careful in your handling of jealous criticism from your leaders, or from those older than yourself. Show them proper respect, but don't let them put you off from following your dream.

Most of the Christian leaders I know are delighted when a younger person under their care begins to show promise of a gift-level beyond their own. They encourage him, they give him opportunity to exercise his gift, they do all they can to stretch him in it.

Sadly, some leaders are the opposite. When they find someone better educated, more sensitive to the Spirit, a more fluent speaker or in any way more gifted than themselves, they feel threatened. Their first reaction is to point out his weaknesses (often very real ones), then to 'humble' him by keeping him down and refusing him opportunity to exercise his gift.

In so doing, such men seal their own doom. Blessing never attends jealous leaders. Their own ministry begins to shrivel and they overcompensate by shouting louder, repeating themselves more often and indulging in other all-too-obvious means of maintaining their precarious position.

What do you do in such circumstances?

First make sure that you have assessed their motives correctly. They may be men of God who are reining you in, not out of threat, but because your character hasn't yet caught up with your gift, and they don't want to turn loose on the local church an insensitive hothead, even though you may be a gifted one.

But if jealousy is clearly evident, start with a frank yet loving approach: 'Charlie, I sense that you're constantly keeping me down. You pick holes in everything I do, and you seem determined to prevent me from playing any useful role in the church. Could I ask you why that is?'

By the time the conversation ends, you should have a clearer idea of whether to stay or move on!

One thing is certain: you will not be able to remain a loner for long, pursuing your dream in isolation. If you are truly walking with God you will know that he wants you established in local church life somewhere, under the care and direction of more mature men of God. Look for somewhere to put down your roots.

The Pain of Disappointment

Yes, opposition from people is tough. But perhaps even tougher is *being let down* by them. If hatred is hard to endure, disappointment is worse.

Disappointment, however, is par for the course in the death of a dream. Every person used by God seems to go through it. Jesus certainly did. He poured his time and effort into the Twelve for three solid years. Then at his arrest, when he most needed their support, they all 'deserted him and fled' (Matthew 26:56). Peter even denied knowing him!

It was the same with the apostle Paul. The sad catalogue of those who forsook him and turned against him can be found in 2 Timothy 4.

Joseph, too, had his share of disappointment. In his case it was chiefly with his fellow-prisoner, the cupbearer to King Pharaoh. This man had a dream while in prison, and Joseph gave him an interpretation that was music to his ears and, what's more, proved correct to the last detail: he was to be freed and given back his job!

Understandably, Joseph asked the cupbearer, on the day of his release, to put in a word with the authorities on his behalf, feeling sure that he would be more than glad to do so in return for such an outstanding favour. Joseph was innocent, after all, and had already languished in prison for a considerable time.

Scripture's sad record reads: 'The chief cupbearer, however, did not remember Joseph; he forgot him.' And Joseph was still in prison two full years later.

Nothing hurts like disappointment. Have you been let down in this way? Have people upon whom you have leaned for support in the fulfilment of your dream suddenly withdrawn their support, leaving you in an emotional heap on the floor, like a cripple with his crutches kicked from under him?

'God deliver us from fair-weather friends,' we cry, often in vain. They become sharp instruments to put our dream to death, and it hurts. But don't despair! Though they must carry responsibility for their action, God is nonetheless in it for our ultimate good. Yes, for our good!

In God We Trust

What should be our attitude under such pressure? Quite simply, *lean on God, who* has promised, 'Never will I leave you; never will I forsake you,' and hold on to your dream.

That's what Jesus did. To his disciples he prophesied, 'You will leave me all alone. Yet I am not alone, for *my Father* is with me' (John 16:32).

That's what Paul did. 'At my first defence,' he wrote to Timothy, 'no-one came to my support, but everyone deserted me . . . . But *the Lord* stood at my side and gave me strength' (2 Timothy 4:16-17).

That's what David did when his own henchmen not only turned against him but even talked of stoning him: 'David found strength *in the Lord his God* (1 Samuel 30:6).

And that's what Joseph did. Concerning his whole, painful prison experience, with its disappointments and all, Scripture records that *'the Lord* was with him' (Genesis 39:20-21).

Don't allow the hurt to turn you bitter. Don't allow resentment to fester like an untended sore. Don't lash out and defend yourself by dragging through the mud those who have opposed or disappointed you. Just lean on God!

God will never let you down. When you hear him say, 'My son, give me your heart'

(Proverbs 23:26), you can give it with confidence, for in the final analysis he, and only he, is the rock of your salvation, the one unshakable foundation for living.

Certainly God wants us to trust other people, love other people, work with other people and depend on other people. But if you stake *everything* on other people and they let you down, your whole life crumbles. So give your heart – the foundation of your being – to God alone. Then, if the worst happens on a human level, you will still have a lifeline to the throne of grace.

All the great characters we have mentioned endured both disappointment and opposition. Their dream died in the arms of their fellows. But they all made it in the end. Their dreams did eventually find resurrection and glory. So too will yours – if you will trust God and hold on!

CHAPTER 4

The pain
of waiting

The difficulties caused by circumstances
and people, great and wearisome though
they are, remain small compared with the
greatest obstacle of all to the fulfilment of
your dream. And what's that? In a word:
delay!

One keen Christian, anxious to grow in his
walk with the Lord, was heard to pray,
'Lord, my greatest need, as you know, is for
patience. So grant it to me, please, and if you
don't mind, Lord, I'll have it *now'!*

We can cope with anything but waiting.
Life, after all, is so very short and the need of
the world so great. Time is of the essence. So
when God gives us our dream we all make
the mistake of expecting the fulfilment now
– if not sooner!

Instant Prophet?

Ray was a typical case. A lively and sociable young man of 17, he was sold out for God and desperately keen to know his will. When he spoke to me, about six years ago, there was a sparkle in his eye and a note of excitement in his voice.

'Guess what?' he enthused. 'At the meeting last night the Lord spoke to me directly through two specific words of prophecy. The gist of them both was that he was calling me to the ministry of a prophet and that I'd be used mightily to stir up his people and further his purposes. Marvellous, isn't it!'

Marvellous indeed, and I had no reason to doubt that this was truly God's word to him. Certainly it accorded with my own convictions.

Straight away, however, I could see what his biggest problem was going to be. He was all set to grab his camel-hair coat and leather belt, switch to a diet of locusts and wild honey and head for the desert armed only with study Bible and notebook. He expected to be proclaiming God's word from pulpits and platforms throughout the land by the end of the week at the very latest!

Firmly, yet kindly, I pointed out that this

was unlikely, that his ministry would grow steadily from small beginnings, that his dream would take *time* to be fulfilled.

What I had to say didn't make me his most favourite person, but, to his credit, he listened and received it. Marriage has done a lot for his character since then. So has getting stuck into the nitty-gritty of local church life. Gradually his ministry is developing and sharpening. He'll be an outstanding prophet in time.

God is in No Hurry

God isn't in any hurry. To him, a thousand years are like a single day. Time and history are firmly in his grasp, and a quiet confidence in his timing on your part will serve his purpose better than nail-biting anxiety and premature attempts to see the dream fulfilled.

Your own dream, like Ray's, will in all probability have to drown in the sea of delay before it springs to life again. It is through faith *and patience,* remember, that you will inherit the promise (Hebrews 6:12).

I've already described my early convictions about God's call on my own life. My wife and I expected to be in full-time Christian service overseas within 12 months of our marriage, and I took a temporary teaching job to make ends meet in the meantime. Believe it or not, I was still in that 'temporary' job *14 years later!*

Fourteen years, I can assure you, is a very long time indeed. So what went wrong? I can answer that in one word: *nothing!*

If anything was wrong at all, it was not in God's wise dealings but in my own impatient expectations. We have instant coffee and instant cake mix, so why not instant dream-fulfilment?

The answer is simple: because that just isn't God's way.

I can't even begin to describe the puzzlement, the frustration, the heart-searching and self-doubt that came in waves throughout that 14-year period. Had I got it wrong? Was my dream just wishful thinking after all? Perhaps the cynics were right and I hadn't really heard from God? Surely things would have moved by now if the dream had been truly from heaven?

The voice of Satan mingled with my own musings: 'Silly fool, you're deluded! Crazy, youthful idealism, that's all your so-called dream was. Forget the whole thing. Just settle for cynicism and mediocrity like every-body else and save yourself a lot of hassle. I've got a pretty tight grip on the world any-way, so no heroics from also-rans like you will bring revival.'

The Funeral of Your Dream

Have you heard similar whisperings within yourself? The dream on which you pinned so much expectation is undergoing a quiet funeral. The devil is giving the oration, and on the coffin is a plaque: 'The mortal re-mains of a dream killed by delay.'

Is that your condition? It is? Then take heart, because you're in good company and, by Bible standards, everything is going ac-cording to plan!

How long did Jesus have to wait for his ministry to begin? Well, let's assume that by the age of 12 the dream had formed, which seems reasonable from the account of his visit to the temple at that age. He began his public ministry at 30 – that's 18 years later. And in one sense his true ministry began only after his ascension, with the pouring out of the Spirit at Pentecost. So that would make it nearer 21 years.

But what about Paul? Surely he dashed straight off after his dramatic conversion and became a mighty apostle, didn't he?

No. He certainly began preaching in the synagogues right away, but it led him into danger. Maybe this was his premature attempt to fulfil the dream that the Lord had implanted in his heart through Ananias: 'This man is my chosen instrument to carry my name before the Gentiles and their kings and before the people of Israel' (Acts 9:15).

Paul soon went off to Arabia, then back to Damascus, where he stayed three years before going up to Jerusalem to get acquainted with Peter. Next he visited his home town of Tarsus, remaining several years in the area before being brought by Barnabas to Antioch, where the two of them taught for at least a year.

All this was part of Paul's training for his coming apostleship, which he actually embarked upon *nine or ten years after his conversion!*

Patient Patriarchs

And what about Abraham? He had to wait about *a quarter of a century,* with natural hope dying by the minute, before Isaac came to birth.

And our friend Joseph? A little calculation reveals that his dream was fulfilled, when his family bowed before him, *23 years* after he first came down to breakfast with his excited account of the wheatsheaf dream.

And Moses? He was stuck with his sheep-farming in the back of beyond for no less than *40 years* before God said, 'Now's the time Moses. Go to Pharaoh and tell him to let my people go.'

So delay in the fulfilment of a God-given dream is apparently quite normal.

Now what about yourself? How long have *you* been smarting under the pressure of delay? However long it may be, rest assured that God certainly hasn't overlooked you. He loves you still and the dream he planted in your heart *will* find fulfilment – in his good time.

So lay down your carnal scheming. Let the dream die so that it can spring to life again in God's time and in God's way.

CHAPTER 5

God's purpose in it all

Adverse circumstances, people who let you down and the pain of delay – these, we have seen, are the 'what' of the death of a dream. Now we must turn from the 'what' to the 'why'.

Why does God allow things to 'go wrong'? Why does he permit you to be frustrated time and time again?

I want to suggest four good reasons, and the first one is: *to test your faith.*

God wants to know how serious you are about this dream. He wants to see whether or not you are convinced it came from heaven.

Are you going to ask and keep on asking for its fulfilment, to knock and keep on knocking – for 40 years if necessary – or are you going to knock on the door a couple of times and, if there's no immediate answer, shrug your shoulders with 'I was mistaken, there's nobody in' and go home? Joseph could have done that many times – but he didn't!

Your Dream on the Test Track

Everything of value is tested.

Gold is heated in a furnace before being certified pure for jewellery-making. Prototype vehicles are driven thousands of miles over the vicious terrain of the test track before a model finally goes into production. Your knowledge acquired in school is put to the test in the examination room before you are considered fit for the more demanding world of work. Future success and usefulness depend on passing the test.

It's hardly surprising, therefore, that God puts your faith to the test. If your whole future is to be based on the conviction that God implanted this dream in your heart, the conviction must be tested.

I wouldn't want to trust my life and safety to an untested vehicle. Neither will God entrust his purposes and reputation to men and women with untested dreams.

Only when your faith has endured the right amount of battering from adversity, opposition, disappointment and delay, and still comes through shining, will God begin to give fulfilment to your dream. Believe me, it's worth it in the end, so hold on!

How to Endure the Test

'It's all right saying hold on,' you reply, 'but what does that mean in practice? *How* do I hold on?'

James has some sound advice here: 'Consider it pure joy, my brothers, whenever you face trials of many kinds, because you know that the testing of your faith develops perseverance. Perseverance must finish its work so that you may be mature and complete, not lacking anything' (James 1:2-4).

Notice that he doesn't say '*if* you face trials', but '*whenever*'. Coming up against setbacks is not something we are spared just because we are Christians. Were God to overprotect us from setbacks, we would be robbed of the chance to benefit from them.

'There's gold in them thar hills!' exclaimed the prospectors in the Gold Rush.

Notice the word 'in'. The gold rarely lay as great, sparkling nuggets on the surface; it had to be extracted from the earth with pick and shovel, and with no small effort. Outwardly, the hills were just boring old hills, but the gold- diggers looked at them with X-ray eyes, so to speak, and saw the treasure lying hidden beneath the surface.

Setbacks are the same. On the surface they look like boring old problems and difficulties, like layer upon layer of earth burying your dream, but spiritually trained eyes can see potential treasure lurking beneath. That's why we can 'consider it pure joy' when we meet them.

Peter puts it this way: 'These [trials] have come so that your faith – of greater worth than gold, which perishes even though refined by fire – may be proved genuine' (1 Peter 1:7).

So when your dream's fulfilment seems remote, and gigantic problems block the way forward, hold on by saying, 'Well, praise God, here's another chance to walk by faith and not by sight. Lord, this setback doesn't surprise me. I regard it as just another test of my faith, and I want you to know, Lord, that I'm never going to let go of my conviction that you planted the dream in my heart. I *know* it will come to fruition one day.'

God likes that!

Meat on Your Bones

The second reason why God allows the death of your dream is *to develop your character.*

Character is what you are. It's the essential you, when all the veneers are stripped away and every 'image' blasted.

Character is what you are when you're alone, acting naturally in the presence of God, uninfluenced by other people.

Character is the measure of your likeness to Jesus Christ, and so high does it rate in God's order of priorities that he will do anything to develop it.

Never confuse character with gift. At 17, Joseph undoubtedly had unusual gifts of leadership and administration, but he lacked the character to match. That's obvious from the way he boasted about his dreams, paraded before the family in his special robe and told tales about his brothers. Characterwise, in fact, he was an immature little creep!

God wanted to put some character-meat on this young fellow's bones. He therefore allowed his dream to die, the special robe to be snatched away and the protective hand of his father to be removed. There's no place like the pit of adversity for turning a little creep into a man of calibre!

You may have outstanding gifts, but without character to match, you will be a liability rather than an asset to the kingdom of God.

Would a father give his two-year-old a loaded revolver to play with? Never! A toddler doesn't have the maturity to handle such a potentially dangerous object. Neither will your heavenly Father give you full scope to exercise your powerful (and potentially dangerous) gifts until you have grown up in character. He wants you to *build* his kingdom, not inadvertently shoot it down through lack of maturity.

God also has an eye to the future. He knows that when your dream is eventually fulfilled, you will have to face pressures far greater than today's, for to be in the vanguard of God's purpose is to be a constant target for enemy attack. That's why, in his wisdom, God is grooming you for that day by educating you in the school of adversity now. He disciplines the sons he loves, for their ultimate good.

Joseph had no idea how tough it was going to be at the top. But God knew, and eased him in gradually with a touch of fright, separation from his family, a period of slavery, a strange culture and language in Egypt, a difficult apprenticeship in Potiphar's household, sexual pressure, false imprisonment and a sprinkling of dashed hopes. That would show what the boy was made of!

And Joseph came out shining. He emerged at the end as a man of character, fit to be entrusted with the leadership he had dreamed of. The jewel of his gift was finally mounted in the gold setting of his character, to make a beautiful and harmonious whole.

Training Time

The host of character benefits to be found in adversity are not for everyone, but only 'for those who have been trained by it' (Hebrews 12:11). Let yourself be trained.

'And how do I do that?' you ask.

First, *curb your natural tendency to grumble* when adversity comes. You know the kind of thing I mean: 'Oh no, not another problem! Why do these things always happen to me? I thought God was supposed to love me. Oh dear, I'm fed up with the Christian life, with my dream, with everything. I think I'll go and eat worms.'

'OK, I'll nip grumbling in the bud. What next?'

'Consider it pure joy.' That doesn't mean a ridiculous pretence that you are delighted with the problem. Any setback to your dream isn't pure joy at all; it's usually pure misery. But what you have to do is *consider* it pure joy.

That means focusing your spiritual gaze on the hidden treasures in the problem and making *a declaration of intent.*

Your declaration might go something like this: 'Well, Lord, I want you to know that I love you and trust you, even in this unexpected setback. What's more, Lord, I'm going to exploit this situation for all its potential blessing. I'm determined to grow stronger through it. I'm going to tackle it with faith and good sense, for your glory, for my own benefit, and to give the devil a poke in the eye.'

Make your declaration out loud, even if you happen to be alone at the time. It will do you a power of good and reinforce your faith just to hear your own voice saying it.

Then *act wisely and sensibly* in the throes of the difficulty, and *keep praising God* in it all. That way, you will grow fast.

Every such testing of your faith, James reminds us, will develop perseverance – an essential character trait of the godly. And perseverance will in turn, and in time, produce the spiritual maturity you so much need.

God is the Tailor

God, then, is in the death of your dream. Don't worry; he knows how much pressure you can take (1 Corinthians 10:13). 'Temptation and tests,' observes Jay Adams, 'are tailor-made to each individual; and God is the Tailor'. Take the opportunity, then, to develop that godliness of character on which your dream's fulfilment can be safely built.

For myself, those 14 years of waiting were a vital period of character building. I slowly learned the art of sociability, at which I was initially hopeless. In my school-teaching I learned how to relate to children with a background and culture totally different from my own. I learned the discipline of hard work. I learned how to be answerable to my boss.

I also learned how to settle disputes, how to cope with depression and boredom, how to handle awkward people, how to have the courage of my convictions and how to discipline myself.

Most of all, through being married I learned how to relate to women in general – that's 50 per cent of the population! Marriage is a wonderful school for character training!

Perhaps I was a slow learner, one of God's remedials, since it took so long to prepare me for the dream's fulfilment. But better late than never!

Now let's recap. We have looked at two reasons why God appears to let your dream die: *to test the reality of your faith,* and *to develop your character.* We shall consider another reason in the next chapter.

In the meantime, are you still in God's school, still waiting? Make the most of it and don't despair. The dream will have its resurrection morning when the time is right!

CHAPTER 6

Another blessing in disguise

Isn't it great to be the centre of attention? Be honest now – it really is, isn't it?

Did you know that some people fall sick and take to their beds just because it's a sure way of attracting a bit of fuss and recognition? Our subconscious need for attention is so great, it seems, we will do almost anything to satisfy it.

How marvellous when someone goes beyond the usual, 'Hi! How are you doing?' to look us in the eye and ask some *genuine* questions about our welfare. And it's even more marvellous when they go on to say, 'Now what can I do to help you? Is there any responsibility I can take off your hands, or any job I can do for you? I just want to serve you in any way I can.'

But why, I wonder, is it so hard for us to adopt the same serving attitude towards others?

Examine your dream for a moment. When you picture its fulfilment do you visualise people noticing you, admiring you and serving you? As likely as not the answer is yes.

I'm sure Joseph's thoughts tended that way. Imagine his daydreams. In comes Reuben, the eldest of the brothers.

'Oh, hi Joseph! I'm glad I managed to catch you on your own. I just wanted to say that, even though you're so much younger than me, I do recognise your superior gift. Dad was quite right to start grooming you for leadership of the family. And, by the way, if there's anything I can do for you – you know, any little humdrum task I can take over to free you up for more important things – just say so and I'll be delighted to help out.'

Or perhaps Simeon: 'Hold it, Joseph. Just stand still a minute. Yes, I thought so, there's an unsightly crease in your robe. Ruins your appearance, it does. Just slip it off and I'll go and press it for you. No, of course I don't mind! It's a real pleasure to be of service to the up-and-coming head of the family.'

Knuckling Under

Here we can diagnose a third reason why God allows things apparently to go wrong and the vision to die – another blessing in disguise. It is *to teach you how to serve others.*

Only the man who has learned to serve others can handle *being* served without its going to his head. So if the dream involves your being in any position of authority, this lesson is essential. Until you have proved yourself capable of being *under* authority you will be unfit to *exercise* it.

The centurion who spoke to Jesus in Matthew 8 understood this principle perfectly. 'I myself am a man *under* authority,' he said, 'with soldiers under me. I tell this one, "Go," and he goes; and that one, "Come," and he comes. I say to my servant, "Do this," and he does it.'

Notice that he didn't say, 'I myself am a man *in* authority'. He emphasised being *under* authority. It was because he himself was willing to be commanded by his superiors that he had authority to command his own servants and soldiers. The authority came down the line from Caesar, through the various ranks within the Roman army, to the centurion, and he in turn represented those higher authorities to the men under him. Or, to turn the illustration on its head: they served him because he served those above him.

Here is a vital principle for you to grasp if ever your dream is to be realised. The Christian who wants to command everybody and be served by everybody, but be answerable to nobody, is a liability in the kingdom of God.

'I follow Christ' (1 Corinthians 1:12)

'But I'm answerable to the Lord Jesus,' you may reply. 'I serve him gladly and willingly, so surely that qualifies me to be in a place of leadership, doesn't it?'

Not necessarily. You *are* answerable to the Lord Jesus, it's true, but he is in heaven, whereas your own life and ministry take place here on earth. And the earth is full of *people* – people you must learn to live with, and some of whom you will be answerable to, under the Lord.

Inevitably, at some point, you will have to find your place in relation to other people who are serving the same Lord as yourself.

And even putting aside specifically Christian relationships, there are people like bosses, school-teachers, tutors and civil leaders whose positions of secular authority require that you adopt a right serving attitude (see Colossians 3:22-24; Romans 13:1-7). There's no escaping people!

Jesus walked this pathway. Before he gained the service of his 12 disciples and the group of women who cared for his material needs while travelling, he spent 30 years as a servant himself – working for Joseph in the carpentry business and later caring for his widowed mother.

Jesus didn't resent it. He never said, 'I'll be glad when all this serving of others is over so that I can sit back and let people serve *me* for a change.'

No, even when he had entered fully into his ministry his attitude was still: 'The Son of Man did not come to be served, but to serve' (Matthew 20:28). Though there came a time when others did serve him, he himself always remained a servant.

You too are called to serve, both now and in the future. There will be no end to your serving. You will never graduate from it. Serving, you see, is not a stepping-stone to greatness – it *is* greatness. So whatever the fulfilment of your dream might mean in terms of receiving the admiration and service of others, you yourself must always remain a servant.

Hard Lessons

Sadly, the serving spirit is so unnatural to human nature that it takes a long time to develop, and God starts his training programme during that frustrating time that we have called the death of a dream.

For me as a teacher it meant learning to serve my headmaster and the education authorities. What was even harder, I had to serve children! I also had to bow to the wishes of my fellow-teachers when majority decisions were reached that I personally disliked.

Then, of course, I had to serve my wife! It took me a long time to recognise that my personal welfare, in addition to our welfare as a couple, lay in my honouring her, caring for her, watching out for her interests and leading her by serving her. A man's wife, I discovered, is largely what he makes her. And what she is in turn governs his own growth.

As for Joseph – poor fellow! – if most of us receive an education in serving, he had a crash course! Suddenly snatched from his favoured position as Daddy's special boy, he had to knuckle under to the wishes of those no-nonsense traders who carried him to Egypt. There, he had to submit to some hard-bitten slave merchant until he was bought by Potiphar.

Even then he had no let-up. Being the newest slave in Potiphar's household, he would no doubt be put upon by all the rest. All the dirty jobs would come his way, especially since he was at a disadvantage in not knowing the language and culture too well. I wonder how often he wept himself to sleep?

Nothing daunted, however, Joseph bowed to the authorities that God had permitted to enter his life, determined to learn true servanthood.

Later, while an innocent in prison, he served the prison warder. He even waited upon his fellow prisoners. By this time he was serving not because he had to but because he wanted to. It was all vital training for the man destined to become Number Two in the land, and before whom men would eventually shout, 'Make way!'

How is *your* serving attitude?

How to be Humble

If it was true of Jesus that 'God exalted him to the highest place', it was only because he first 'humbled himself and became obedient' (Philippians 2:8-9). Could it be that God hasn't yet exalted you to the place your dreams portray simply because you haven't yet learned to humble yourself and become obedient?

Does the pride that resents serving still linger in your heart? If it does, remember that 'God opposes the proud but gives grace to the humble' – a verse important enough to appear three times in the Bible (Proverbs 3:34; James 4:6; 1 Peter 5:5).

'OK, I do need more of a serving spirit. I do need to be more humble. But how on earth do I go about it? Do I start wringing my hands and grovelling like Uriah Heep?'

Please don't! But you are correct in recognising that humbling is a do-it-yourself job. Scripture makes it clear that we ourselves do the humbling, while God does the lifting up: 'Humble *yourselves,* therefore, under God's mighty hand, that *he* may lift you up in due time' (1 Peter 5:6). James agrees: 'Humble *yourselves* before the Lord, and *he* will lift you up' (James 4:10).

Don't ask God to humble you. You could regret it. Do it yourself!

'And how do I do that?'

First, *be a worshipper.* To worship the Lord is to lift him up, to exalt him, and thus automatically to humble yourself by comparison. There's no such thing as a proud worshipper.

Today's emphasis on praise and worship isn't just the current fad. God himself has inspired it, not only for his own glory but as a means by which his people can humble themselves, receive more grace and so be prepared for his service.

Second, *be quick to say thank you.* I take it for granted that you will do so to the Lord, but please express your thanks and appreciation also to other people, no matter how small the favour they have done.

Why? Because every time you express your thanks you lift that person up and acknowledge yourself to be the recipient of his help, and that is to humble yourself.

Do you find it difficult to say thank you? Then face the fact that ugly pride is the cause. Be quick to repent, then set out to find any possible excuse for expressing your thanks to all and sundry.

Third, *surrender your 'rights'.* Follow the

example of Jesus, who 'did not cling to his privileges as God's equal' (Philippians 2:6 J.B. Phillips) but gladly let them go. What about your supposed right to a better job, a steady income, a little self-indulgence, a husband, a wife, a car? Let such rights go. Then, if you are privileged to receive these things, regard them as gifts of God's grace – a stewardship rather than a right.

Self-humbling of this variety will enable you to lend your car to someone else without anxiety or to rejoice genuinely when someone else is promoted.

Fourth, and again following our Lord's example, *look out for the interests of others.* If Jesus could take 'the very nature of a servant' (Philippians 2:7), so can you. And what does that mean in practice? It means *looking for jobs that need doing and doing them!* How gloriously spiritual!

Some jobs will match your special skills. If you are a trained carpenter, who better than you to mend the wobbly chair-leg for the old lady across the street?

But don't stick at that. Go for jobs that a prouder person would consider beneath him. Do you have an advanced university degree? Then volunteer to give those harrassed parents a morning off by taking their energy-packed youngsters to the park on Saturday morning.

What were Jesus' qualifications? He was the unique, mighty Son of God. And what task did he choose to do on one occasion? He washed the disciples' feet, those horny, dusty feet stained with grass and camel dung. Thus he humbled himself. 'I have set you an example,' he said, 'that you should do as I have done for you' (John 13:15). Humble yourself by serving.

Fifth, *be a good employee.* Your boss might be a veritable slavedriver, but the fact remains that he is your boss, and Scripture is abundantly clear in requiring you to work both reliably and hard for him (for example, Ephesians 6:5-7; Colossians 3:22-24; Titus 2:9-10; 1 Peter 2:18).

Dreaming of You

Imagine your boss lying in bed in those half-asleep moments before lapsing into slumber. He is mentally going through all his staff, and the furrow on his brow deepens as he pictures the slackers, the moaners, the sycophants and the hypochondriacs who work for him alongside you.

Then *you* come to mind. Ah, what a contrast! A smile replaces the frown on his face as he pictures you. 'If only the rest of my staff were half as loyal, respectful and hardworking, I'd be a truly happy man!' he murmurs as he slips beneath the surface of sleep.

Exaggerated, you think? It shouldn't be. I'm not suggesting that you become a spineless yes-man who takes a masochistic delight in being trampled on by a tough and uncompromising boss. But I *am* suggesting that you review your work attitudes in the light of Scripture, because here is a powerful means of self-humbling which God will honour.

So look out for the danger signs pointing to bad attitudes: competing for the boss's recognition and being jealous when others are promoted; an inflexible attitude which makes you complain at any changes he proposes; seeing the whole job as just a convenient temporary step in the outworking of your personal aspirations.

Instead, look for ways to increase your efficiency. Work hard at every task you're given, especially the ones nobody else wants. Look upon an awkward boss as a tool in God's hand to bring out spiritual qualities and mature attitudes in you.

From there, it will be a small step to submission in other departments of life. You will quickly learn, for example, to be submissive to those older than yourself (1 Peter 5:5) and to spiritual leaders in the church (Hebrews 13:17). Service will become a way of life.

So Far, So Good

Where does all this leave us in the pursuit of our dream? We have already seen that God allows it to die in order *to test our faith* and *to develop our character.* In this chapter we have pinpointed a third reason: *to teach us how to serve others.*

Is this a lesson you still have to learn? Then go for it – simply become a servant! Humble yourself by being an ardent worshipper, by being quick to say thank you, by surrendering your 'rights', by looking out for the interests of others and by being a good employee.

That will leave you free to consider the fourth and final reason why dreams are allowed to die, which is the subject of our next chapter.

CHAPTER 7

Jumping to conclusions

Now for the final reason why God lets the dream die: it is *to shake out your preconceived notions of how it will be fulfilled.*

While the *essence* of your dream is from God, the chances are that the details will eventually work out in a manner quite different from what you expect. Clear you may be on the 'what' of the dream, but the 'how' remains God's business.

This was certainly true in my case. The call to full-time Christian service was undoubtedly from God. So was the conviction that I would bless many of God's people internationally. At that point, however, the God-inspired element came to an end and my own active imagination took over.

Wild Imagination

It is usually here that our problem lies: we are so anxious to see the basic dream fulfilled that our imagination runs riot in anticipating the details of *how* it will happen.

For me, the word which caught me out was God's promise that I would be a blessing to his people *internationally.* What word immediately comes to mind when you think of Christian service overseas? That's right – *missionary.* Surely, I thought, this was the way the dream would be fulfilled!

The way we imagine the future is inevitably governed by our past and present experience – the company we keep, the books we read, the training we receive from parents and teachers. More than likely, however, God has plans for your future that will break the mould of previous experience.

In my Brethren background we had no full-time ministers or pastors, so clearly that avenue of service didn't figure in my thoughts. But we did have a strong missionary interest, and my avid reading of the exploits of David Livingstone and Hudson Taylor had been supplemented over the years by the accounts of overseas service delivered at scores of missionary meetings.

So what else could God be calling me to but to missionary work?

A Missionary Calling?

At the age of 18 I went off to university to study Spanish language, history and literature for three years. There I became fascinated with Latin America – especially Peru. The Quechua- speaking descendants of the ancient Incas became my major interest, a once proud nation now living in material poverty and spiritual blindness.

With my linguistic ability I would soon be able to communicate with them in their own language, I felt sure, and they would quickly be turning to Christ in droves. All I had to do was accumulate a few prayer partners and get out there as fast as possible once my studies were completed!

In the meantime I got involved with the university Christian Union and, as missionary secretary, soon found myself inviting missionaries on furlough to come and talk to the C.U. about their work.

Though I had to invite speakers from a broad cross-section of countries, my particular leanings gave me a bias towards those with a Latin American connection. One such lady, I recall, worked for the South American Missionary Society and was based in, of all places, Peru!

No-one gave more earnest attention to her talk than I did. What's more, her gentle and soft-spoken manner appealed strongly to me since I myself was of a reserved personality. She was living proof that you didn't have to be loud and extrovert to achieve something for God.

At the end of her talk she appealed to us students to stay alert to the needs of Peru and to consider seriously whether the Lord would have us make ourselves available for missionary service there.

As you can imagine, I fell for it, hook, line and sinker. This, I thought, must surely be the final confirmation regarding the out-working of my youthful dreams: *God was calling me to evangelise the Peruvians!*

I Got it Wrong!

Though I didn't realise it at the time, I had put two and two together and made five. I had simply got it wrong!

It wasn't that the missionary lady was a

ruthless pressuriser of youthful emotions. On the contrary, she was measured in her re-counting of the need, and utterly sincere in her conviction that each individual's call must come from God.

The trouble lay not in her but in me. By al-lowing my mind and feelings to dwell on the dream's outworking in too much detail, I had laid myself open to being misled.

And so the dream had to die. All the frust-ration of knocking in vain on the Peruvian door, the puzzlement over our domestic cir-cumstances that kept us at home, those long years of school-teaching – all were neces-sary to rid my mind of the preconceived no-tion of what the calling of God would mean.

Most probably *you* have it wrong, too.

Look upon your present difficulties as God's way of purging your heart of the fanci-ful ideas (all very spiritual, of course) that get in the way of *his* plans for you. The kernel of your dream is from God. The husks are your own imagination.

Even Great Men Make Mistakes

Don't despair! You are in good company yet again, because our friend Joseph had the selfsame problem. The essence of his dream of leadership was unquestionably heaven-born, but his idea of its outworking was way off track.

Let's spy on his imagination again.

'Ah yes, things are really looking up now,' he reflects with a smile. 'Twice today Dad has complimented me on my good sense, and he did it in front of my brothers, too, bless them. I'm "wise beyond my years", he said. Well, far be it from me to question his opinion!

'I'm really looking forward to next week. Dad's going to introduce me to his account-ing system so that I can learn to handle the family finances. It all looks very promising.

'Yes, I can visualise it so easily. Dad calls a family conference. All of us take our places, sitting in order of age – except me, of course. "I've called you together today for a very special reason," Dad will say. "As you can all see, Joseph isn't sitting where his birth position would place him – the eleventh son out of 12 – but he's right here at my side. This should give you a good idea of why we're here.

'"Of all you boys, Joseph has consistently shown himself superior in terms of initia-tive, leadership ability and practical com-monsense. I indicated this some time ago when I gave him the special robe he's wearing.

'"But now the time has come to give more permanent form to my conviction. I therefore officially declare Joseph to be my primary heir. Reuben, normally this would be your privilege as the eldest, of course, but I'm sure, not only that you've recognised Joseph's superiority as clearly as I have, but also that you're more than willing to go along with my decision."

'"Oh yes, absolutely, Father."

'"Good. Well, from now on I'll be taking more of a back seat and handing over the reins of everyday family affairs into Joseph's capable hands. See that you give him the respect due to him."

'From there, it'll be a walkover,' muses our hero. 'I'll soon have the family affairs licked into shape. Then I'll find myself a wife and get to grips with my own domestic life. And there'll be no financial worries, of course, since the major part of Dad's property will come to me as his primary heir.

'Once I'm nicely established I should soon be able to extend my influence in the district and eventually achieve countrywide prominence. In fact, with youth and ability on my side, I'm bound to become a really outstanding patriarch, dispensing my blessings upon everybody wise enough to bow to my leadership. Yes, the sky's the limit, Joseph, old son, and thanks to God's help you're flying high already!'

God's Way is Best

Never in a thousand years could Joseph have foreseen what actually happened. What an incredible story! And what a far cry from the story he had imagined!

The sobering thought is this: it took over 20 years of the death of a dream to shake out his preconceptions so that God could fulfil the dream *his* way.

The course of my own life was equally unexpected. Never could I have foreseen that my local church would progress the way it did; that respected brothers in the Lord would eventually ask me to join them in full-time pastoral work – not in Peru but in my own home town; that I would get involved with a Christian magazine and set up a Bible college course; that I would travel overseas to minister the Word of God and in a host of different ways – *God's* ways – see the original dream fulfilled.

I certainly never imagined I would be writing this book! And the saga isn't over yet. The future is exciting!

In the light of this chapter, then, what fanciful ideas is the Lord shaking out of you? Whatever they are, let them go. *Let* the dream die, so that he can bring it to life his way. He knows best!

CHAPTER 8

Making the most of the interim

The most important time of your life is *now!*

Yesterday, with both its successes and its failures, is past and gone for ever. And tomorrow? Well, you have hopes and expectations, of course, but the fact remains that tomorrow is as out of reach as yesterday. So what does that leave?

Today!

'But surely this whole question of dreams points us forward to the future, doesn't it?'

Yes, but any consideration of the future forcibly turns our gaze back on to the present. You can't start building a wall in mid-air; each brick rests on the one laid before it. In the same way, it is only on the foundation of today that your tomorrow can be built.

Today, and only today, is here now, yours to mould and shape as you will.

The car driver whose eye searches too far down the road ahead is the one who fails to see the red traffic signal right under his nose. Along with the driver who gazes too long in his rear-view mirror, he is likely to find himself in a pile-up.

It's not a bad thing, of course, to keep an eye on the road ahead and to keep glancing into the mirror, but in the end the driver with the keenest awareness of his *present situation* is the one most likely to arrive safely.

There's a lot to be said for casting a glance in the rear- view mirror of your life from time to time and rejoicing in God's past goodness. 'I remember the days of long ago,' said the psalmist; 'I meditate on all your works and consider what your hands have done' (Psalm 143:5).

It's not a bad thing, either, to have an eye to the future, pressing forward, like Paul, to the things that lie ahead (Philippians 3:13-14). Indeed, we must, for don't the very dreams we're considering together lie in the future, at least as far as their fulfilment is concerned?

But the mark of the Christian who is going places is that his legitimate backward and forward glances are never permitted to weaken his conviction that the most important time is *now.*

The Importance of Attitude

Your dream is not yet fulfilled. Today is yet another day in the interim – that seemingly endless period that we have called the death of a dream. Where, then, do you go from here? How can you make the most of today, for tomorrow's sake?

Begin by examining your *present attitudes.* Why? Because without right attitudes to today there can be no fulfilment of your dream tomorrow.

So what are the right attitudes to cultivate?

For starters, *put your heart into your current responsibilities.* Here we need to underscore the lesson of chapter six, because for most people their major current responsibility is their daily work, and for some reason they regard it as both unspiritual and unrelated to the fulfilment of their dream.

'What job are you in at present?' I asked one young man who aspired to Christian leadership.

'I'm working in a bakery,' he replied, adding, with a shrug of the shoulders, 'It's long hours and terribly boring. I hate it really, but it brings in enough money to live on.'

That young man would never be fit for Christian leadership as long as his attitude remained unchanged. The job was unimportant to him, an unfortunate necessity to be endured on the fringe of his life. That kind of passivity is always the enemy of progress.

Godly Enthusiasm

No matter how dull and uninspiring your present occupation or situation, no matter how far removed it may seem from the dream in your heart, no matter how unfulfilling or alien to your natural inclination, *throw yourself into it with enthusiasm!* That's the will of God!

'But you don't understand; my future isn't in this,' you may retort.

To which I would reply, 'So what? Act as if it were!'

Let the interim be filled with success, so that when you leave the job – if that is what the Lord wants – you do so in a blaze of glory, not with the feeble phut-phut of a damp squib.

Potiphar had never known a servant of Joseph's quality. Neither had the prison warder ever met an enthusiast who threw himself so wholeheartedly into every jailhouse job. It wasn't that Joseph envisaged his entire future as lying in household service or being a prison 'trustee', but he nevertheless reached for the top in both. His eye was on the *Top Slave of the Year* award until he went to jail, when the *Outstanding Jailbird* trophy took his fancy!

For myself, I never saw my future in school-teaching. How could I, when another dream was steadily burning in my heart? Nevertheless, in the absence of any other immediate prospect, I decided to give the job everything I had.

After a few years I had just about exhausted the possibilities of that particular post, and someone suggested I should try for a promotion.

'Oh, no,' was my response, 'I don't see my future in teaching, so what's the point of climbing the career ladder? As long as the job provides my bread and butter, that's all that matters.'

On reflection, however, I realised that without some sort of new challenge I was in danger of growing stale, and God never uses stale men and women. He likes them fresh and sharp!

So I began to push promotion doors and found myself in a series of teaching jobs which kept me constantly on my toes, the final post being the deputy headmastership of a large school, with every prospect of a headship before long. 'But weren't you in danger of being taken over by teaching and losing sight of the dream?' you may ask.

No, I never lost sight of the dream. Making the most of the present job or situation must not be viewed as incompatible with the call of God. It is possible to give yourself enthusiastically to present responsibilities and still know that your future lies elsewhere.

Hard work and enthusiasm now, even in the most painful of jobs, is in fact the only sure foundation for success in your future calling. 'God has made me fruitful in the land of my suffering,' declared Joseph (Genesis 41:52). You can choose to have the same testimony – the operative word being 'choose'. If you want to see your dream fulfilled, choose to make the most of today.

You are Not Alone!

There's another key to milking the interim of maximum blessing: *remember that God is with you!*

Is that hard to believe just now? Well, it's true all the same. 'Never will I leave you; never will I forsake you' remains God's final word on the subject (Hebrews 13:5). He will be with you to no greater extent when the dream finds fruition than he is at this moment.

'But if God is with me, why are things so slow to develop, and why are so many things apparently going wrong?'

We have already looked at those questions, and by now you shouldn't be needing to ask them. It is to test your faith, to develop your character, to teach you how to serve others and to shake out your preconceived notions of how the dream will be fulfilled. For now, just rest in the truth of God's promise that he *is* with you.

What's more, he's with you to *bless* you! That's the kind of God he is, committed to encourage and prosper you because he loves you. Nothing you do or achieve in the future, not even the development of a mighty ministry, is going to cause him to love you any more than he does now.

Believe it, even though the circumstances might suggest otherwise.

'The Lord was with Joseph and he prospered . . . . The Lord was with him and . . . gave him success in everything he did' (Genesis 39:2-3). That was the testimony of Joseph, not when he ruled Egypt but when he was still labouring as a *slave* in Potiphar's house!

Nothing changed even when things took a turn for the worse. 'While Joseph was there in the *prison,* the Lord was with him . . . and gave him success in whatever he did' (Genesis 39:20-21, 23).

Faith Makes it Work

It's important for you to see that this success of Joseph's was not automatic. It was a faith issue. Success came about because, even in slavery and in prison, Joseph *believed* that the Lord was with him.

Faith always expresses itself in action, and Joseph's response to the conviction that God was still with him was seen in his rising to the challenge of those difficult circumstances and working hard.

Let's spy on him again. It's 6am on yet another day of yet another seven-day working week, and bleary-eyed Joseph is standing in the courtyard with his fellow-slaves as the hard-faced supervisor allocates the work.

'OK, you foreign trash,' he yells at Joseph. 'Mucking out the stables for you today. Get to it!'

Potiphar was more than a one-horse officer. He had strings of the animals, and mucking out was an endless task – one to which Joseph seemed to be permanently assigned by the less than sympathetic supervisor.

For a moment he felt rising within him a strong urge to moan, complain, stamp his feet in anger and vent against God his total frustration. Then his faith rose to the surface.

'Well, glory to God, here we go again! You *are* with me, Lord, and I'm going to give those wretched stables a mucking out of the highest order – getting right into the corners and leaving the place fit for Potiphar himself to live in, never mind his horses. Egypt's going to see that when a man of God gets on the job, things begin to look up!'

Joseph went whistling to his work,

strengthening himself in the Lord, day in, day out, month in, month out, sustained by his rock-steady conviction that, in spite of everything, God was with him.

The Response of Faith

God is with you, too – right here and now. How far you benefit from the fact depends, however, on your response to it. Paul the apostle, for his part, saw God's love and grace as a massive incentive to hard work (see 1 Corinthians 15:10). How about you?

Give yourself fully to your present job. Work with God's grace. Let the unbelievers see your reliability, your integrity, your frankness, your good humour. Overcome evil with good.

In this chapter we have pinpointed two attitudes to cultivate in the interim between now and your dream's fulfilment: *Put your heart into your current responsibilities* and *remember that God is with you.*

No matter how grim your situation, stick with it unless or until the Lord clearly moves you on. Ultimately you will be able to testify, as could Joseph, that the Lord made you fruitful in the land of your suffering.

CHAPTER 9

Practising
for tomorrow

The Field Marshal of tomorrow is the little
boy who marches up and down, wooden
rifle over his shoulder, playing soldiers
today.

Here we have a third key to making the
most of the interim: *practise the ultimates on
a small scale now.* Whatever your dream
points towards, look for opportunities to live
it out in principle today.

Are you called to full-time evangelism?
Then share Christ with your workmates
now. Are you destined for a great healing
ministry? Then pray today for the sick in
your family, school or factory. Is God calling
you to big business so that you can provide
money to finance kingdom projects? Then

start giving away a good proportion of your present small wage.

'Whoever can be trusted with very little can also be trusted with much' (Luke 16:10). It is now, during the death of your dream, that God is providing you with the opportunity to prepare in a small way for its larger-scale fulfilment.

Cloud-Cuckoo-Land

Remember that your future ministry, when it comes, will not drop out of the blue right into your lap. *It will grow out of what you are doing now.* Unfortunately, many Christians fail to see this vital connection because in their minds the present and the future are stored in separate compartments. They see no relationship between the two.

An angler may dream of catching a fish, but unless the baited hook is in the water, and the line from the hook connected to his rod, and the rod in his hand, he will catch nothing, no matter how vivid his dreams. Scores of sincere Christians who would reply, 'That's obvious', nevertheless fail to see the connection between their own vision for the future and their activity here and now, and continue to live in a superspiritual cloud-cuckoo-land, out of touch with reality.

'I believe God is calling me to full-time evangelism,' says one who, when questioned, admits he has never really spoken about his faith to anyone, let alone led someone to Christ. His 'call to full-time evangelism' belongs to a faraway land of make-believe, more akin to a fairy tale than to life in the real world.

It's like believing that, when Jesus returns, we will be like him, but making no attempt here and now to deal with our vile temper in the power of his Spirit. Or enthusing about 'taking the city for the Lord' when our church hasn't numbered more than 40 people for ten years and we carry on in the same old routines as before.

If your dream is indeed from God, you will make a practical connection between it and present reality. Your conviction of the dream's origin will *impel* you to start acting in line with it today – and every day.

A Leader Among Slaves

That's how Joseph operated. He was called to leadership. Household slavery wasn't exactly what he'd expected but he determined to earn leadership even in that humble setting. So he grafted away and worked his way up the leadership ladder in Potiphar's house.

Prison life was even further removed from his ultimate expectations but he resolved to take responsibility even there, and to earn it by serving both the prison warder and his fellow-convicts.

As Joseph thus proved faithful in little, God was in due course to trust him with the future of a whole nation.

You believe you will one day lead a church of thousands? Make sure, then, that you effectively lead the mini-church of your own wife and children today.

'Oh, come on. Don't be so earthy, man. I'm talking about a big church with thousands of people, making an impact on the community and shaping the decisions of local government. I'm talking about programmes of teaching and ministry, about a team of prophets stirring the folk to action, about mutual love and commitment, about the presence of God among us in signs and wonders. Don't talk to me about my wife and children. My wife has moods and my children have tummy upsets and nightmares.'

The fact is, the church of thousands will be made up of people who have moods, tummy upsets, nightmares and a host of problems besides. A man who can't shepherd three or four family members into greater wholeness will never do it for a multitude. True Christianity doesn't run away from the real world of the here and now; it masters it.

'Tall oaks from little acorns grow', states the old proverb. 'Take care of the pennies, and the pounds will take care of themselves', declares another. Stay in touch with reality and begin to act now in line with your dream.

How Can I Bless You?

Now here's a fourth attitude for the interim: *concentrate on blessing others.*

The dreams of the self-centred are never fulfilled. That much Jesus made clear when he pronounced, 'Whoever wants to save his life will lose it.' In the present context that means *don't be forever talking about your dream.*

Some of the hardest people to cope with, I

find, are the very artistic types, who are often unpleasant simply because they're so self-centred. They always seem to be talking about '*my* art', '*my* work', '*my* creativity', '*my* artistic integrity'.

God doesn't want you to be a spiritual 'arty type'. In other words, don't ramble on about your dream, your future ministry, your programme, your spiritual ambitions, your vital part in the eternal scheme of things.

Trust God to work out the dream for you. He doesn't need you to be dropping hints to other people and boring them to death in the process – because to be self-centred is inevitably to be a bore.

Constant talk about your spiritual ambitions indicates a heart full of pride, for it is out of the overflow of the heart that the mouth speaks (Luke 6:45). Spiritual success chased after in a proud, self-centred manner will never be achieved. Like the bar of soap in the bath, the harder you try to grip it, the further away it jumps.

The First Move

Concentrate instead on other people. The world's twisted principles are stood on their head in the kingdom of God. The man who receives is the one who has first given away. The woman with lots of friends is the one who has first shown herself friendly. The Christian most blessed is the one who reaches out to dispense the most blessing to others.

Joseph lived that way. The man with such powerful dreams of his own learned to focus on the dreams of others. His caring and warm-hearted invitation to the cupbearer and the baker was, 'Tell me *your* dreams' (Genesis 40:8).

When did you last take a genuine interest in someone else's future? Or do you still prefer to chat endlessly about your own?

Love, taught Paul, 'is not self-seeking' (1 Corinthians 13:5). By definition it is *other-oriented.* It is practical concern for the interests of others at the expense of one's own. You can have the greatest of gifts, both natural and spiritual, and yet for lack of love end up as nothing but 'a resounding gong or a clanging cymbal'. Who wants the ministry of tuneless percussion?

Consider Job. Only when he prayed for his friends, instead of wallowing in self-centredness, did the Lord restore his fortunes. Is his example one you need to follow?

'Whoever loses his life for my sake will find it' is the positive half of Jesus' famous statement in Matthew 10:39. Are you eaten up with your own ambitions? Lay them down. Let the dream truly die in self-sacrificial service to others. That way, and that way alone, God will bring it to fruition.

In this and the previous chapter we have identified four attitudes to cultivate in the interim between the conception and fulfilment of a dream: 1. Put your heart into your current responsibilities; 2. Remember that God is with you; 3. Practise the ultimates on a small scale now; 4. Concentrate on blessing others.

Easier said than done, it's true, but not impossible. With the Lord's help these attitudes (and those to follow in the next chapter) can become yours, moulding your character in readiness for what lies ahead. Go for it!

CHAPTER 10

More attitudes to cultivate

'I love mankind – it's people I can't stand.'

Charles Schulz's famous statement voices the frustration of those who claim to love society but can't stomach real live people. A classic case was Karl Marx, who, for all his social theorising and 'doctrinal' concern for people, couldn't get on with anybody!

Happily, God isn't like that! While he loves 'the world' (John 3:16), he also loves the individual. 'The Son of God . . . loved *me*,' enthused Paul, 'and gave himself for *me*' (Galatians 2:20).

Isn't this exactly why Jesus came? His aim was not to start an organisation, to give us a creed or to provide material for preachers. No, he came to redeem *people!*

People are God's great concern. They matter far more to him than things, doctrines, ideas or disembodied 'truth'. More, even, than angels. And people must be your concern, too, if your dream is ever to be fulfilled.

Here we have a pointer to the next attitude to be cultivated in the interim: *learn to get on with people.*

All Sorts of People

Most of us can cope with people who share our own background and culture but we find it hard to relate to the rest. If your dream is ever to be fulfilled, however, you must learn to get on with *all kinds* of people. God does; you must do the same.

Are you from a rough and ready background? Then you must learn to relate to people with Ph.D.s who speak with a cultured accent, without being threatened by them. If you grew up in a wealthy home and enjoyed an academic education, it is vital to learn to be at ease with those less privileged materially and educationally, and to converse with folk less tidy-minded than yourself. Introverts must learn to get on with extroverts, aristocrats with labourers, and vice versa.

The traditional barriers of sex, race and colour have to be overcome. Men and women – especially those with emotional hurts from dealings with the opposite sex – have to learn to get along together. Blacks, whites, Asians and orientals must rise above the racial differences of skin colour and culture, for 'here there is no English or American, black or white, Indian or Jamaican, middle class or working class, Jew or Arab, Ph.D. or E.S.N., but Christ is all, and is in all' (Colossians 3:11 – author's own version!)

Jesus shows the way. He could hold his own with the shrewd Pharisees and with Nicodemus the intellectual but was equally at ease in the company of 'tax collectors and sinners' – the riff-raff of his day. Wealthy Zacchaeus received no more of his attention than did the loose-living woman at the well.

Jesus wasn't embarrassed by babies and little children; he took them on his knee and blessed them. He enjoyed the social life of weddings. He just liked *people!*

Conversation with the King

We can also take a leaf out of Joseph's book. In his long personal interim he learned to get on with both slaves and slavemasters, with wealthy Potiphar and his well-to-do visitors, with the tradesmen who came to the house, with fellow-prisoners – with all types.

The ultimate test of Joseph's social education came when he was suddenly whisked from his prison into the presence of the mighty Pharaoh. Far from being tongue-tied and ill at ease, he found he could talk naturally and easily in his presence, combining frank speaking with due courtesy. By contrast, he could also show sympathy and understanding towards his rascally brothers when they later came grovelling at his feet.

How do you get on with people? It's an art that can and must be cultivated by all who would be used in the service of God. The dreams of the social misfit will never materialise.

For me this was a major area of need. I loved doctrine, books (Berkhof's *Systematic Theology* was bedtime reading!), ideas, the Word of God, theories – but I couldn't stand people. They were useful for preaching to, of course, so long as they didn't expect to involve me in their social chit-chat afterwards!

Changing in this respect involved long and painful spiritual surgery. The surgery was followed by physiotherapy – every time

I began to slip back into anti-social attitudes the Lord used to twist my arm! At one stage I sat down and drew up a list of questions that couldn't be answered by 'yes' or 'no' so that I would be able to survive in the world of small talk. Now you understand why it took 14 years to realise my dream!

While I'm still happy to be alone – and indeed need it from time to time – I love people now. I find deep fulfilment in being with them and helping to meet their needs. So be encouraged – if the oddity that I was can learn to get on with people, there's hope for you!

Seduction in Egypt

It is in one particular aspect of human relationships – relating to the opposite sex – that Joseph shows us yet another interim attitude: *the practice of moral integrity.*

There is immense power in purity. No-one given to lax morals can realise his dream of usefulness in God's kingdom.

The sensual focus and earthy pressures of the godless society in which we live will provide ample scope for leaning on God in this area. Satan knows that if he can just lure you into sexual sin – especially if it can be made public – your testimony as a Christian is ruined for years to come. The increasing number of God's servants falling this way is ample evidence of the success of Satan's policy.

Potiphar's wife, being a wealthy woman with a host of servants, probably had nothing to do all day but make herself glamorous. But for whom? With her husband away for long periods on military duty, the good-looking young house-servant was an obvious target.

We should not underestimate the force of her approach to Joseph. It was brazenly direct: 'Come to bed with me!' What's more, it wasn't an isolated assault on his moral integrity: 'She spoke to Joseph *day after day'*. Worse still, it was frighteningly hard for him to avoid because the very nature of his household duties meant that Joseph couldn't avoid meeting her. And being a slave, he didn't have the option of leaving that employment for another.

In their own way, your own moral temptations are likely to be just as strong. Face them the way Joseph did. He first recognised that to give in would be to sin *against God* (Genesis 39:9). Then he flatly refused the sexual proposition. He was also wise enough to put himself out of the reach of temptation whenever possible: 'He refused to go to bed with her *or even to be with her*' (Genesis 39:10). And when it came to the crunch, as she made a grab for him, he took the only sensible course: he 'ran out of the house' (see 1 Corinthians 6:18).

This was the man whom God eventually honoured not only by fulfilling his dream of leadership but also by giving him a beautiful and high-ranking woman to be his wife.

Have you mastered your sexuality, or has it mastered you? It makes a good slave but a tyrant of a master.

Remember that your sexuality is God-given. Don't fall into the idealistic error of pleading with the Lord to take away your sex drive, because he won't do it. To grant your request would be to rob you of a vital aspect of your humanity. The answer lies in spiritual control, not spiritual castration!

You can do it. 'His divine power has given us everything we need for life and godliness' (2 Peter 1:3). Practise purity and sexual integrity if you would see your dream fulfilled.

CHAPTER 11

. . . And yet more

By now you are beginning to see the importance of *character* for those who would serve God. The attitudes suggested for cultivation between now and the realisation of your dream are designed to build Christian character. They touch on what you *are* rather than what you *have* by way of gift or ability.

Character formation takes time and is the main reason for the 'delay' factor considered in chapter four. But the duration can be reduced by your active co-operation with the Lord in the learning of the vital lessons. We have highlighted six of those lessons so far. In this chapter we suggest two more. Together, they should keep you going for a while!

The Extra Mile

Here, then, is the seventh attitude to cultivate: *give beyond what is expected of you.*
The Christian with dreams must learn to go
the extra mile.

It's 6.20 in the evening and our meal is
over. As I lounge in the armchair with one
eye on the television news and the other on
the evening paper, I feel a pleasant lethargy
creeping over me. My wife, meanwhile, is
taking the dirty dishes into the kitchen. It's
her privilege to see to all that, I console myself.

Then the Holy Spirit reminds me that hus-
bands are to love their wives 'as Christ loved
the church', that is, self- sacrificially. So, by
an act of will, I drag myself out of the
armchair, stagger through to the kitchen and
insist on washing up.

With the job done, I feel very virtuous as I
look at the dishes stacked on the draining
board. I've done the dirty work now; my
wife will dry them later on.

Then the Holy Spirit starts preaching his
'extra mile' sermon. 'Why don't *you* dry the
dishes? Yes, I know your wife said she
would do them later on, and I know there's
no obligation upon you, but wouldn't it be

good to do it anyway?'

So I reach for the tea-towel and respond to the appeal. Five minutes later, all the dishes stand shiny dry, lined up on the table. Boy, do I feel virtuous now!

I'm just about to wander back into the lounge when the Holy Spirit's after-meeting begins.

'Come on, why are you leaving the dishes on the table? Surely, having gone so far, you might as well finish the job by stacking them away in the cupboard.'

I groan inwardly. 'Look, Lord,' I argue, 'I've already gone the extra mile by drying them. Are you seriously suggesting yet another extra mile? A three-mile hike is a bit much after a hard day's work, you know.'

But in my heart I know there's no arguing with the Lord, and the dishes are soon stacked in the cupboard where they belong.

How down to earth can you get! Situations like that seem far removed from the dream that inspires you. How can there be even the remotest connection between the two?

The connection is in fact both real and vital. Most of us need some of our idealism knocking out of us, especially if, like Joseph, we are dreamers. It is in the school of hard knocks, of kitchens, dishes, awkward bosses, dull routine and everyday responsibility, that 'extra mile' character is formed.

No Escape!

Don't try to run away! Escape from one set of tailor-made teaching circumstances will lead you into another set where the Lord plans to teach you exactly the same lesson. 'It will be as though a man fled from a lion only to meet a bear' (Amos 5:19)! Only when you learn to give beyond what is expected of you will God move you a step nearer the fulfilment of your dream.

Are you doing the very minimum that is required of you in your office, factory or school, while all your energies are channelled into chasing your own spiritual ambitions? Let the ambitions sink down into the grave where they belong, and leave their resurrection to God. In the interim, learn to be an extra-miler, a going-beyonder, a giver.

Surely this was the key to Joseph's success as both slave and prisoner. He gave Potiphar the maximum, not the minimum. Later, instead of sulking in his prison cell, he set about improving the quality of life for both the warder and his fellow-convicts. He could have got away with a lot less, but he chose to give more.

Going beyond what was expected of him eventually became a way of life, so that when at last he stood before Pharaoh he was not content just to give a straight interpretation of his dreams, as requested; he went on to give some unsolicited advice about how to prepare for the famine that the dreams foretold.

Become a giver yourself. Give your time, your efforts, your skills, your money. Go the extra mile. Prepare yourself for greatness.

Let God be God

Now here's the final attitude to cultivate in the interim: *stay open to the supernatural!*

We have remarked already on the folly of preconceived notions of how your dream will be fulfilled and the wisdom of leaving it with God. To leave it with God means it will come about supernaturally, for he is the ultimate controller of both people and circumstances.

Don't try to help him. Nothing is more certain to set back the fulfilment than frantic efforts on your part to make it happen.

That, you may recall, is exactly the mistake that Abraham and Sarah made. To receive the promise of a son was one thing; it was something else altogether to produce one when Sarah was long past childbearing age. So they tried to engineer the fulfilment of the promise themselves.

It was a tragic mistake. Abraham fathered a son, Ishmael, by Sarah's servant-woman, but this wasn't the son of God's promise. Isaac, when he came, was born *supernaturally*. His conception and birth were nothing less than a miracle.

Moses, sensing the call of God to deliver the Israelites from Egyptian bondage, messed it all up by interfering in disputes, killing an Egyptian and burying his body in the sand. Forced to flee for his life, Moses found that God had a school-house in the desert of Midian, from which he graduated after a 40-year course and went on to deliver Israel God's way – supernaturally.

Joseph thought he had made it when he strutted around in his special robe, telling tales on his brothers. Little did he know of the far greater role to which God was calling him – one to which he was brought by the divine manipulation of circumstances, not by his own efforts.

Don't try to engineer the fulfilment of your dream! The dream was conceived by God. Let him also be the one to bring it to birth – supernaturally, when the time is right. Don't burden yourself with an Ishmael.

Hold on, by all means, to the *essence* of your dream, but leave the detailed outworking in the Lord's hands. In the meantime, practise the principles we have outlined in these chapters: 1. Put your heart into your current responsibilities; 2. Remember that God is with you; 3. Practise the ultimates on a small scale now; 4. Concentrate on blessing others; 5. Learn to get on with people; 6. Practise moral integrity; 7. Give beyond what is expected of you; 8. Stay open to the supernatural.

As you learn the lessons on the divine curriculum, keep an eye open for the unexpected, supernatural intervention of God.

'The one who calls you is faithful and *he* will do it' (1 Thessalonians 5:24).

CHAPTER 12

The dream fulfilled

When the time is right, God moves fast!

One moment Joseph was languishing in prison with no glimmer of release in sight; the next moment the key was grating in the lock and an official was handing him shaving gear and a change of clothing, with the words, 'Get moving, you have an audience with Pharaoh in 15 minutes'!

It was the same with Moses. After 40 years of routine family life and sheep farming, he was taken completely by surprise by the call of God at the burning bush: 'Now, go. I am sending you to Pharaoh to bring my people the Israelites out of Egypt' (Exodus 3:10). His dream burst out of the straitjacket of faded hopes into sudden, violent reality. God's time had come!

God's time will come for you, too. And most likely it will be when you least expect it, when your hopes have faded almost – but not quite – into non-existence.

'Ah, wonderful!' you murmur. 'What a time that will be! All the patient waiting behind me, all the struggles past and gone!'

Don't you believe it! Certainly it's a marvellous thing to break into a new era of fulfilment in the purpose of God, especially when it's something you have long waited for and dreamed about. But it's no walkover. If you have a glamorised picture of what it will mean, permit me to prick the bubble of fantasy.

Don't imagine that when the breakthrough comes you will cruise automatically into unbroken blessing, power and effectiveness. Some of the toughest times of my life came *after* my entry into full-time Christian service – and they are still coming! We may graduate from God's school, but thereafter we find ourselves in full-time 'higher education', where the course is tougher, the demands more stringent – and the satisfaction deeper.

Challenges Ever Greater

The servant in Luke 19 was given one mina by his master and told to put the money to work, which he faithfully did. His pleasure was to be able to say, 'Sir, your mina has earned ten more.'

His master's reply is instructive. 'Well done, my good servant! Because you have been trustworthy in a very small matter, take early retirement with a fat pension, free food and drink and a villa by the Mediterranean.'

No: 'Because you have been trustworthy in a very small matter, *take charge of ten cities.'*

The reward for his work was greater work! Trading with the one mina had doubtless brought its worrying moments, its pressures, its joy and its satisfaction. Now he was to face, in running ten cities, whole new dimensions of worry, pressure, joy and satisfaction. But having by now learned how to handle worry and pressure, a greater proportion of his soul was left open to relish the increased joy and satisfaction!

Now you can see why it is so vital to learn the lessons of the interim. Without those under our belt, the heightened pressures of the dream's fulfilment would crush us. But having learned them, we discover within ourselves a faith and a capacity not only to cope with, but also to rejoice in, whole new levels of adversity, disappointment, delay and opposition, because we know how to meet them with faith.

Joseph, after his interview with Pharaoh, found himself burdened with a weight of responsibility way beyond anything he had previously known. He was Number Two in the nation! As for Moses, the hassles encountered with the people of God must at times have made him yearn for the company of sheep again! But both men not only survived – they thrived!

We too, when we prove faithful in little, are entrusted by the Lord with much. That's how it will be for you in the realisation of your dream: more of everything, especially the thrill of being used increasingly in the working out of God's great purpose. Each step forward with him brings a unique pleasure. We sense that, instead of being a mere dagger in his hand, we have now become a broadsword which he wields to make deeper inroads into the ranks of the enemy. What pleasure that brings!

This, then, is to be the pattern for the rest of your life: more lessons, more learning, more faith, more maturity of character, more work, more responsibilities, more joy, more fulfilment.

Lesser Longings Satisfied

I have observed, too, that there are unexpected bonuses in the resurrection of a dream. One is that *God graciously takes care of our lesser longings.*

For Joseph, these must have been twin desires: the longing for a wife and the yearning for freedom of movement. His last memory of the outside world was that of the seductive advances of Potiphar's wife, stirring desires for the legitimate sexual fulfilment of marriage which imprisonment was then to deny him. And as for freedom of movement, that had been denied him from the time his brothers first sold him into slavery.

When his dream began to be fulfilled, however, both these needs were met almost incidentally: Pharaoh immediately gave him a wife, and the nature of his new responsibilities meant that Joseph 'travelled throughout Egypt' (Genesis 41:45-46). God is wonderfully gracious to those who bow to his will!

Centuries later, Solomon dreamed of enjoying outstanding wisdom and discernment. God gave it, and for good measure threw in the riches and honour that any new king would naturally desire (1 Kings 3:12-13).

For myself, I had always fancied a Volkswagen car – preferably a brand new one. Not the mightiest of ambitions, you may think, but a real one nonetheless! After coming into full-time ministry, the prospects of owning such a car seemed remote, especially as I took a 50 per cent cut in salary.

Shortly afterwards, my father, who himself does not drive, said he would like to buy a car. I would keep it and run it in return for chauffeuring him and my mother from time to time.

It seemed like a great idea! Had he any particular car in mind, I enquired?

'Yes, I thought maybe a new Volkswagen.'

By the end of the week I found myself behind the wheel of a brand new Passat, hardly believing my luck. Luck? No, the loving provision of God. He's like that!

My God, Solomon's God, Joseph's God is also your God! Trust him to fulfil your dream. Trust him also with your lesser longings.

The Dream Keeps Growing

But the best bonus of all is that *the dream grows.*

You need never fear suffering the fate of that great man of war, Alexander the Great, who is reported to have sat down and wept because there were no more worlds to conquer. God, who knows we will always need something more to catch our imagination and spur us on, will provide it. You will never die of boredom in the kingdom of God!

My dream has grown. At first I saw my coming into full-time pastoral work as the fulfilment – which it certainly was. God used me to the blessing of many. Some overseas visitors spent time in our church before returning home, carrying a blessing with them. Surely this was it!

But then the dream began to grow.

I soon found myself involved with and eventually editing *Restoration* magazine, which at the time of writing goes out to over 80 different countries. Later I was privileged to set up and teach in a leadership training course which has equipped men and women of God for ministry in every continent. I have had the privilege of preaching the Word of God in Scandinavia, the USA and Africa. Then the whole dimension of writing came into view, a dimension I'm currently exploring with great satisfaction.

What lies in the future I don't know, but I do know it will be an ever-expanding experience of the original dream. Something inside every one of us yearns for constant increase. To be in the will of God is to find it.

'Of the *increase* of his government and peace there will be no end' (Isaiah 9:7). Here is a promise which holds good not only for the progress of God's kingdom in the world but also for our personal experience.

In the end, you see, your dream and mine are one and the same: it is a dream of *increase,* of knowing God more intimately and being used for his glory more completely. It's just the details that vary. And he's a dream-fulfilment specialist. What a great God we have, who offers such glorious prospects!

Joseph, who once dreamed of the Alpine crags of family leadership, found his dream expanding to Himalayan proportions, until he became the saviour and leader not only of his immediate family but of a whole mighty civilisation. And when he died, at the ripe old age of 110, it was to step straight from his

personal Everest into the endlessly satisfy-
ing mountainscapes of eternity, to enjoy the
dream-fulfilling Jehovah God himself.

The same exciting expectation is yours
and mine! So lay down the fleshly ambitions
that stand in the way of experiencing God's
best. Learn God's lessons. Embrace those
very circumstances that proclaim the present death of your dream. Let the grain fall
into the ground and die so that *God* can
bring it to life in his time and his way, for the
bearing of much fruit.

'The vision is yet for the appointed time; it
hastens toward the goal, and it will not fail.
Though it tarries, wait for it; for it will certainly come, it will not delay' (Habakkuk 2:3
NASB).

God is in control. Hold the dream. Grasp
your present responsibilities. Be strong in
faith. The rest you can safely trust to God. He
never fails!